Start Orienteering

A scheme of work for primary teachers

OBJECTIVES

To introduce
the idea of a map
being a symbolised
picture of the ground

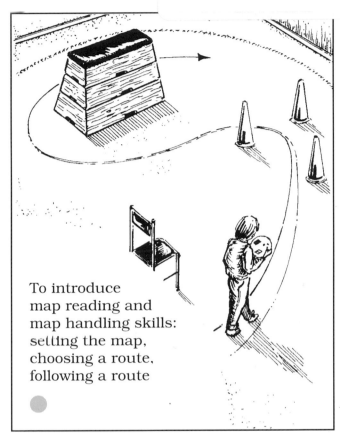

To introduce
map reading and
map handling skills:
setting the map,
choosing a route,
following a route

To use games and
exercises which foster
an awareness of
the sport of
orienteering

To encourage children
to make simple
meaningful
maps

1 DESK TOP PLANS: SHAPES AND RELATIONSHIPS

IN THE CLASSROOM

OBJECTIVES

* *To introduce the concept that maps and plans are a pattern of shapes*

EQUIPMENT
Models of houses, trees and fences
Paper, pencils, coloured pencils/crayons
Coloured paper

KEY WORDS: SHAPES • PATTERN • PLAN • MATCHING

Teacher preparation
Collect landscape models or objects with clear and contrasting shapes

Lesson
1. Place three objects on a sheet of paper in a very simple **pattern**. Draw round each piece then remove the objects to show the outline **shapes**. Discuss which shape **matches** which object and what shape each one is. A **plan** has been produced of the model.

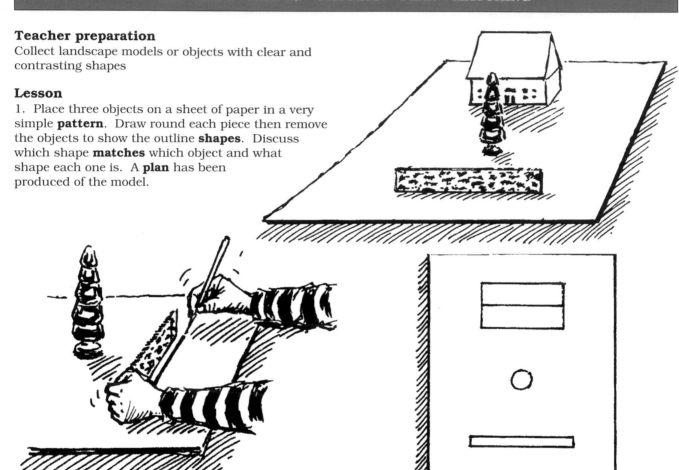

2. Place the objects in a different relationship. Draw the correct shapes on a piece of paper laid next to the models. Involve the children in deciding what shape to draw and where it should go. If the map is to be correct the drawing must match the model.

3. Give out paper and ask the children to draw the correct shapes in the right pattern. Place the objects on a central table, or use sets of objects with smaller groups of children.

4. Find the treasure
Gather the class round the central table keeping the same pattern of objects and each child having their own plan.

The children close their eyes while the teacher puts a cross or 'T' (for treasure) on the paper underneath part of one of the objects e.g. under the corner of a house. The teacher shows the class where the treasure is on the plan by marking on a red circle, then, pointing to the model, asks "Where is the treasure hidden?"

This should be repeated a few times. The **plan** must **match** the model if the treasure is to be found easily.

Next, let the children see where the treasure is to be hidden and ask them to mark on their plans where the treasure is to be found. This again can be repeated.

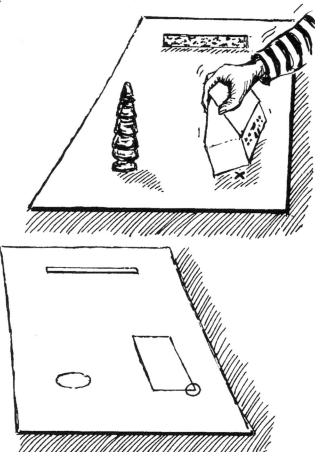

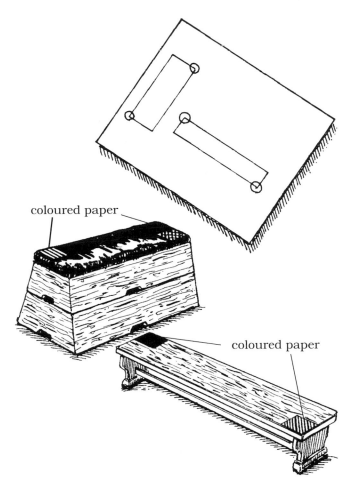

coloured paper

coloured paper

6. Demonstrate that if you rotate your plan, the shapes no longer match the apparatus. When the children have tried this for themselves, ask them to colour in the circles on their maps with the appropriate colours.

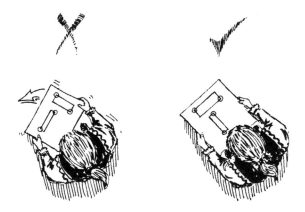

5. In a larger area, lay out two pieces of apparatus or furniture in a clear pattern (above right). The children draw shapes to match. Some children may find this difficult.

Place a piece of coloured paper on one corner of each piece of apparatus. Each child draws a circle on his/her plan to indicate where the paper is. Repeat with three or four more pieces of paper of different colours The children must **match** their plans to the apparatus (i.e. hold them the right way round) all the time.

These games and exercises can be adapted to suit the needs and ability of your particular group of children. For example, the children of a class which understands these ideas quickly could practise walking towards a piece of apparatus from different parts of the area, keeping the plan set as they move.

2 SYMBOLS AND PLANS
PLAYGROUND OR HALL

OBJECTIVE

• *To introduce the use of symbols on maps*

EQUIPMENT
Symbol cards
Twelve pieces of apparatus (box, bench, chairs, cones)

KEY WORDS: SYMBOLS • PLAN • PATTERN

Teacher preparation
Make a set of cards, each with a symbol on it for one of the pieces of apparatus to be used. The symbol should be the same shape as the actual object - just smaller.

Lesson
1. Hold up a symbol card and ask the children to match the shape of the symbol with the correct piece of apparatus. You can point out that the **shape** on the card is called a symbol and is taken from how the piece of apparatus looks from above, and that the symbol is drawn smaller in order to fit it on the paper.

2. Place the symbol cards in a box in the centre of the area. The children run round weaving in and out of the apparatus. On 'whistle' each child picks a card out of the box and runs to a matching piece of apparatus. Repeat a few times.

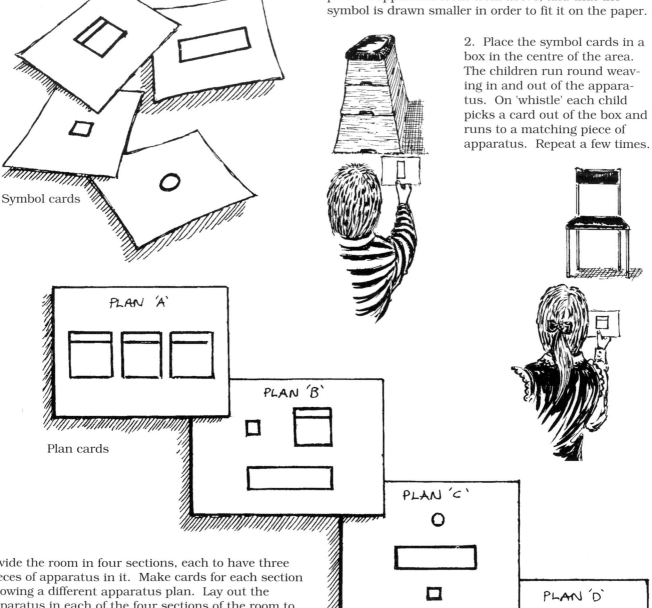

Symbol cards

Plan cards

PLAN 'A'

PLAN 'B'

PLAN 'C'

PLAN 'D'

Divide the room in four sections, each to have three pieces of apparatus in it. Make cards for each section showing a different apparatus plan. Lay out the apparatus in each of the four sections of the room to match one of the plans you have made. You can use some of the children to help you.

3. Show the class the four apparatus plans and discuss which plan matches which pattern of apparatus.

4. The children run round in the area again. The game is to look at the plan selected by the teacher and go to the part of the room with the matching section of apparatus.

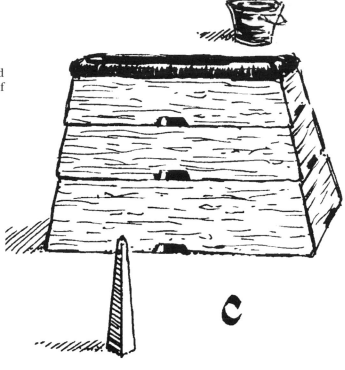

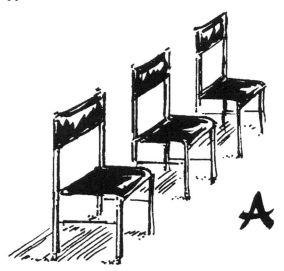

When this is mastered, use two cards at once. The children can be told either:

a. to choose one of the cards and go to the matching section of apparatus or

b. to go to one followed by the other.

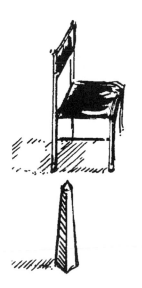

When you hold up a card, select a child to announce which card is being shown. Select children you suspect of following the rest and not thinking for themselves.

*The plan is like a picture. Tell the children to look at the **plan** and imagine how the **pattern** of apparatus will appear.*

Further work

Look at and draw the shapes of a variety of objects as seen from above.

③ SETTING THE MAP
HALL OR PLAYGROUND

OBJECTIVES
- *To reinforce the use of symbols*
- *To introduce the meaning of setting the map*

EQUIPMENT
Copies of a large-scale plan of part of the hall or playground
Five small orienteering control markers or coloured tapes
Five animal pictures

> **KEY WORDS: MAP • SET • CONTROL • SYMBOLS**

Teacher preparation

Make a large-scale plan of part of the playground or one end of the hall. Lay out two or three pieces of apparatus if there are no other features. Make enough copies of the map for each child to have one. Hang five control markers with animal pictures attached to them on distinctive features. Draw red circles marking the positions of the controls on all the maps.

Lesson

1. In the classroom show the children the plan or map to be used. Emphasize symbols, re-inforcing lesson 2. Pick out familiar features and discuss new symbols such as wall, fence, building.

2. Give out the maps with the control circles on. Identify which features the controls are on.

3. Playground/hall
Go to the area and establish a base where all the controls can be seen easily. Place a map on the ground (set). Count together the number of controls that can be seen (5). Count the number of circles on the map (5). Then match each circle with the correct control.

4. Show how easy it is when the map is set so that the features on the map match the real ones around. Move the map in different ways asking each time if it is set or not. Then the children set their own maps. As practice, the children change places with a partner and then re-set their maps.

5. The teacher points to a circle on the child's map. The child then points to the correct control flag. The child visits the control and returns with the correct name of the animal. Repeat until all the controls have been visited. Ensure that the child sets the map and points to the control before leaving base.

6. Collect the controls. Go over what has been learned.

Follow up
Write down the words:
SYMBOL, SET, MAP, CONTROL
Talk about maps in general: who uses them, how, when.

Emphasize their importance for finding your way and following a route

Further activities
Get the children to draw pictures or plans of their own models.

Cut up a school map into pieces to form a jigsaw and practise putting it together.

A TREASURE ISLAND
HALL OR ROOM SPACE

OBJECTIVES

• *To establish the meaning of the word "set" and follow up the use of shapes and symbols*

EQUIPMENT
Paper, clipboards,
Crayons (blue, green, black, brown, red)
Treasure island features e.g. lake (water basin), river (blue rope or cord), house (box), trees (skittles or cones), field (outlined with canes or rope), tracks (chalk lines)

KEY WORDS: MAP • SET • ROUTE

Teacher preparation
Collect equipment. Decide which area to use. Children need to be able to overlook the whole area. Doing the exercise in the playground or large school hall should allow the children to follow their route. Read a story about an island.

Lesson
1. Give out paper, boards, crayons. Seat the children round the area to be used for the island.

2. Using chalk or rope, mark out the coastline of the island in a simple shape and as large as possible. As you add features on the island, the children draw them on their own paper. A mixture of pictures and symbols is quite acceptable for this map.

3. Place large features first: the lake (basin of water) and the river (blue cord) leading to it; the box as the

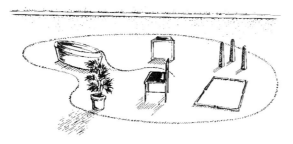

house; the cones (or pot plants) can represent trees; a chair can be a lookout tower. A field can be used to fill in the gaps.

4. Story line
Following a shipwreck a box of treasure is buried. Before being rescued the mariners make a **map** of the island so that the treasure can be found later. The children are the shipwrecked mariners.

Ask the children where they want to bury their treasure. Mark the place with a "T".

Now years later you return to dig up your treasure and land on the island at the point where you are sitting. Mark it on your map with an arrow.

t = treasure

5. "Which **route** will you take to get to the treasure?" The teacher demontrates. Plan the route looking at the model, then trace it on the map with a finger. The map must be kept **set** to follow the route.

A few children can talk through the route which they would follow, identifying the features they will pass by pointing at the model or the map.

6. If the island is big enough, the children can then try to follow the **route,** walking from one feature to the next until the treasure is reached.

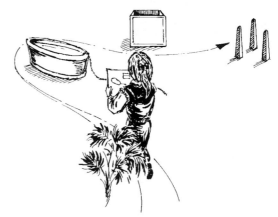

7. Working in pairs. One child with a map and route stands at the side and tells their partner where to go to follow the route, eg. "walk to the right of the tree, turn towards the lake, go round the lake, . . ."

Follow up
Talk about islands. Collect information about islands such as Australia, Britain or Iceland. Make maps of other areas or models
This is an ideal starting point for cross-curricular work

USING TABLE TOP PICTURE MAPS
CLASSROOM

OBJECTIVES
- *To reinforce the concept that a map is like a picture*
- *To see how a map can be used to show and help you follow a route*

EQUIPMENT
Table-top picture maps, coloured pencils
Model houses and trees, a model car
String
Boards to lean on

KEY WORDS: PICTURE MAP • SET • ROUTE • SYMBOLS • PLAN

Teacher preparation
Draw a simple picture map and a plan of a table top model, and make copies, or copy the ones shown on page 15.

Lesson
1. Set up the model to match the map. Give each child a copy of the picture map. The children should stand or sit round the model so that they can relate their picture maps to the model. Ask them to **set** their maps and identify each of the houses and trees. Bear in mind that a picture map is drawn from one side, so looking at it from another side is less easy.

2. Introduce the model car, which is going on a tour, visiting each of the houses. As the car is directed along its **route** the children follow where it goes on their picture maps.

3. Choose a new starting point.
The children now draw in the route the car takes as it goes from house to house. A piece of string showing the route on the model will help them to draw the correct line. Arrows on the line will show the direction the car is going.

4. Give each child a **plan** of the model. Compare and match the picture map and the plan with each other and with the model. Identify the **symbols** showing trees and houses. **Set** the plan. Locate the start point of the route shown by the string and already drawn on the picture maps.

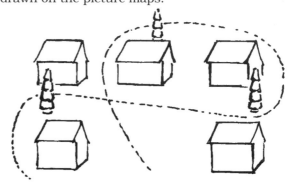

Draw the route on to the plan by looking at the line of the string. Compare it with the line on the picture map.

5. Select individual children to <u>talk</u> through the route shown on the map

Summary
Maps are made up of **symbols**. Symbols are map language. The symbols can be read and seen as pictures of the features they represent. A map can be used to plan and follow a **route**.

Follow up
Children can make their own models and then make picture maps or plans of them. Plot in routes using string, and then transfer them onto the maps.

PLAYGROUND TREASURE ISLAND

OBJECTIVES

• *To introduce moving with the map set*

• *To reinforce that the map is a symbolised picture of the ground*

EQUIPMENT
Box (house), 3 cones (trees), chair (look-out tower)
Rope or chalk (to mark the boundary of the island)
Picture maps of the island
Two sets of plans of the island:
(i) plain (ii) a numbered set with different routes on

KEY WORDS: SET • FOLLOW A ROUTE

Teacher preparation

Make three circle shaped treasure island picture maps. The features should be the same on all, but the picture maps should be drawn as seen from different directions. Make a few copies of each one (in total enough for all the children). Cut out the circular maps. Label each view on the back as a, b, or c. (If preferred, use the example on p. 15). Lay out the box, cones and chair to match the map. Use a rope or chalk to show the outline of the island.

Make a plan showing the same features in the same positions. Copy that too. On four plans add four different routes. Copy so that you have enough in total for each child to have a route map.

Lesson

1. Give each child a copy of one of the three picture maps. Standing round the island, identify the features and point out that a picture map is from one view only. Ask the children to move to that edge of the island which matches the view shown on their own map. You will then have a third of the children on each side of the island.

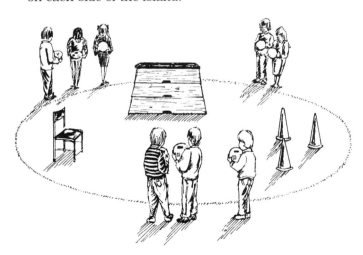

Point out that the picture map will only be useful when you look at the area from the correct side. Move round the outside of the island to check whether their maps match the side they have chosen. If you have time, swap maps and repeat.

2. Exchange the picture maps for the plans . Identify the features. Circle the island again, stopping to set the plan. Repeat several times. Show how the plan can be used from any point round the edge of the island.

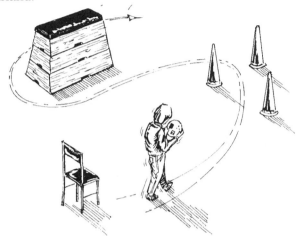

3. Select a child to choose a route to visit all the features on the island. The class follow on their plans the order in which the features are visited. Demonstrate how the map stays 'set' as the child turns and changes direction. "Move your body round the map". Place the 'set' map on the ground and show how the map stays with all the <u>symbols</u> matching, or <u>set</u>, while the child moves round until they are facing the new direction

4. Exchange the plain plans for the route maps. Each child should go and stand on the edge of the island where the triangle is on his/her map. The start points should be spread round the island. Set the map. Look at the route. "Where does it go?" "Can you follow the route?" Emphasise "move your body around the map".

The children now exchange maps and follow another route. Check that they are at the right starting points with their maps set. Number the maps on the back, making 1 the easiest route. This enables you to give the simplest routes to the children finding the exercise difficult. Occasionally stop everyone and check that all maps are 'set'.

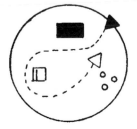 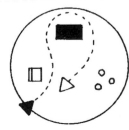 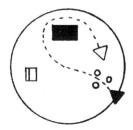 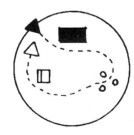

Further work
1. Reading the map as they follow the route
2. Running the routes

ORIENTEERING STAR EXERCISE

OBJECTIVES
- *To introduce orienteering*
- *To find map features (controls) which are out of sight*

EQUIPMENT
Boards size approximately 20 x 20 cm
Maps of the school grounds
8-10 mini-controls or coloured tapes
8-10 coloured wax crayons with string attached
Enlarged copy of map (size approx A3) taped to a board

KEY WORDS: ORIENTEERING • SET • CONTROL FLAGS

Teacher preparation

Plan 8-10 control sites, some within sight and others out of sight of the base/start. Mark the controls on all the maps, including the enlarged version, with red circles (use a circle template). Number each circle. Mark the start with a triangle. Tape the maps to the boards. Hang the control markers and crayons at the controls. Use the same start/base as for lesson 3.

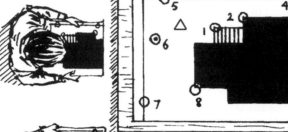

Lesson

1. Give each child a map on a board. Go outside to the base shown as the triangle on the map. Set the map and discuss the features and symbols. The large A3 size map is useful for demonstrating how to set the map.

Identify (point out) a control. Set the map. Teacher and children run to the control. Repeat a few times, checking that everyone can set the map. Use a distinctive wall, hedge or road to help match the map to the ground. Point out the crayon hanging from the control.

2. Star exercise: each child is given one control to find. The child has to go to the control, colour in the right circle on the map with the crayon hanging there then return to base to join the queue ready for the teacher to identify the next control to visit.

Before running off the child should point out to the teacher the control flag he/she is going to, or, if it is out of sight, describe where it is.

Continue until most of the children have all the circles coloured in. Check that the colours are correct.

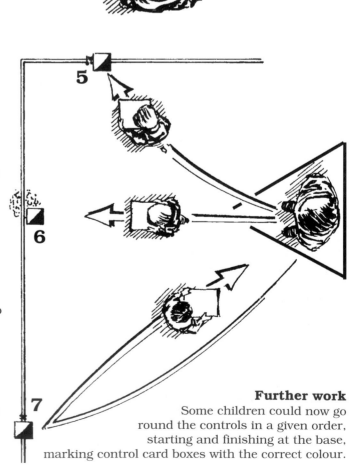

Further work
Some children could now go round the controls in a given order, starting and finishing at the base, marking control card boxes with the correct colour.

POINT TO POINT ORIENTEERING
IN THE PLAYGROUND

OBJECTIVES
* *To remind the children that they should see the map as a picture*
* *To teach moving the body round the map so that the map stays set, and the person faces the direction of travel*

EQUIPMENT
6-8 mini-control markers (or coloured tapes) with wax crayons attached
A large (A3) map of the school and grounds
Small (A5) maps of the school and grounds

KEY WORDS: WALK ROUND THE MAP • KEEP THE MAP SET • ORIENTEERING

Teacher preparation
Plan 6-8 control sites. They should be mostly different from those used for lesson 7. Mark all the control sites on all the children's maps with red circles. Mark the start/finish with a triangle. Highlight a strip down one edge of the map with a bright colour. This need not necessarily be North, rather a hedge or wall which will act as the main reference line for setting the map. Hang the controls and crayons.

Lesson
1. In the classroom: Evaluate the group's understanding of the playground map and the symbols used. Look at the large map of the school and ask individual children to identify specific features e.g "Which entrance do you use to come into the school?"; "Which area is used for play at breaktime?" Ask them to close their eyes and imagine what each feature looks like: "Make a picture of it in your head". This is how they should 'read the map'.

2. Outside: Start at the triangle. Set the map using the coloured edge to help. Lay the map on the ground in front of you still set.

On the map, find the control with number "1" beside it. This is the first control. Walk around the set map until you are looking in the direction of the control as viewed from the start. Pick up the map. The map is set. You are facing along the route you want to follow. DEMONSTRATE CLEARLY. All go to control 1. Do not use the crayon.

Repeat the procedure for control 2, control 3, control 4 . . . finishing at the triangle:

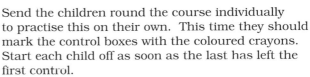

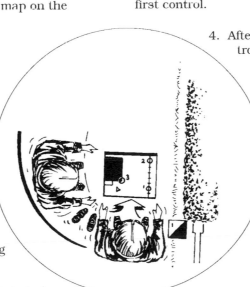

* Set the map (on the ground, if this helps)
* Find the next control on the map. What is it?
* Walk around the map until you are facing the right way.
* Look. Can you see the marker? If not, plan your route.

Send the children round the course individually to practise this on their own. This time they should mark the control boxes with the coloured crayons. Start each child off as soon as the last has left the first control.

4. After each child has visited all the controls in the right order, send him/her round again. This time the circles on the map can be coloured in. The children needing extra help will have been identified by this time, and can be given more attention.

Summary:
This is orienteering!

Further work
Drawing the symbols and writing the name beside each one.

Show a video about orienteering.

Find out when there will be a local event (see p.17 for addresses for information) and send information home to the parents to encourage the family to take part.

⑨ THE GRID
PLAYGROUND

OBJECTIVES

• *To reinforce and evaluate understanding of setting the map*

EQUIPMENT
21 cones
4 corner features (flowers, shrub, chair, rounders post . .)
2 grid maps
  a 4 courses starting from each corner
  b Courses starting from any outside cone

KEY WORDS: MOVE YOUR BODY ROUND THE MAP

Teacher preparation

Lay out the grid of 21 cones and 4 corner features. Space them evenly 3-4 metres apart (3-4 paces). Check that all the lines are straight (like the map).

(flowers) ❁   ◯   ◯   ◯   ✻ (shrub)

◯   ◯   ◯   ◯   ◯

◯   ◯   ◯   ◯   ◯

◯   ◯   ◯   ◯   ◯

(chair) 🪑   ◯   ◯   ◯   ⌲ (rounders post)

Make up the maps (two sets):

One set with 4 different courses of 4 controls each with the Start and Finish at corners (mark the corners A, B, C and D, if this helps). Use a double circle for the Finish

A second set with Starts and Finishes anywhere on the outside of the grid with 6-8 control sites on each course. Ideally there should be a different start for each child (up to 16).

Set 1
Map A

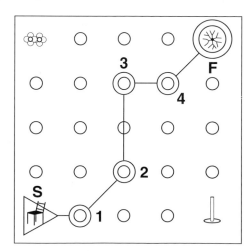

Set 1
Maps B, C and D

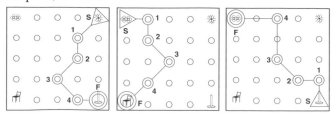

Lesson

1. At the grid, demonstrate the following:
• Start at the triangle (find the correct corner from the grid map).
• Keeping the map set (using the corner features), stand looking towards control 1.
• Walk to control 1. Keep the map set by moving your body round the map.
• Identify, face and look towards control 2.
• Repeat this until the finish.

2. Send the children, with a map each, to find their start corner. One person from each corner starts.
• "First ones: set your map, face towards control 1, walk to control 1.
• Stop, face towards control 2. Are your maps set?"
• Work with this group until they all reach the finish, then repeat with the next 4 (again one from each corner). Children stay where they finish.

Example of Set 2 course

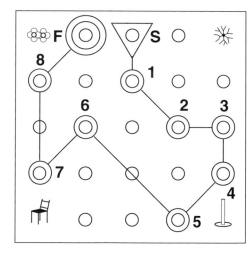

3. When all have done one course, collect the maps and redistribute to new start groups (A - D - B - C).

4. Exchange the first set of maps with the second set. Everyone stands by their start cone. Talk them through each control, or let them try on their own. Help those who need it.

5. The children exchange maps with someone else and start again.

Further work

Let the children plan their own course, follow their own course and swap with others. This lesson can be adapted as the children develop skills and experience: Make the grid larger, with more distance between the cones. Put out a NORTH flag and take away the corner features. Use a clip compass. Make sure the grid is laid out true to Magnetic North/South/East/West.

OBJECTIVES:

- *To evaluate the child's understanding of a map as a pattern of shapes in the correct relationship to each other*

- *To evaluate the child's ability to relate a plan to a model*

- *To evaluate the child's understanding of symbols*

1. Match a plan to a picture (or table top model)

Which plan matches the picture map?

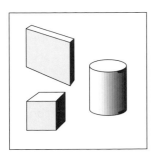

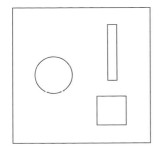

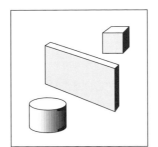

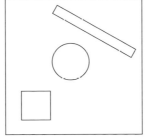

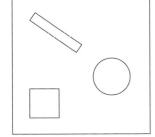

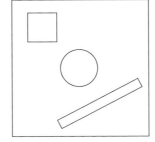

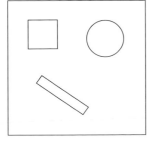

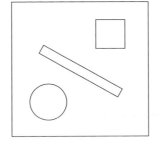

— — — — — — —   — — — — — — —

Answer   Answer

2. Relate a plan to a model

Teacher preparation: Arrange a model of several objects. Make a plan of it and mark a route in a clear line.

"Drive" the toy car round the model along the route shown on the plan .

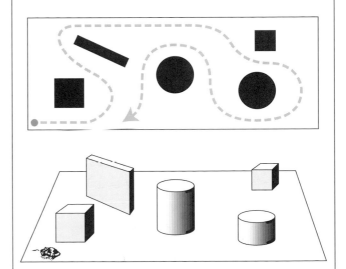

3. Symbols

Teacher preparation: Make several cards showing symbols that appear on the playground map

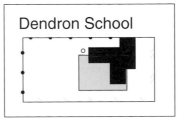

a. Match each card with the same symbol on the map

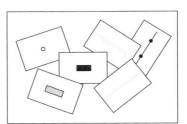

b. Name the symbol

SCHOOL MAPS

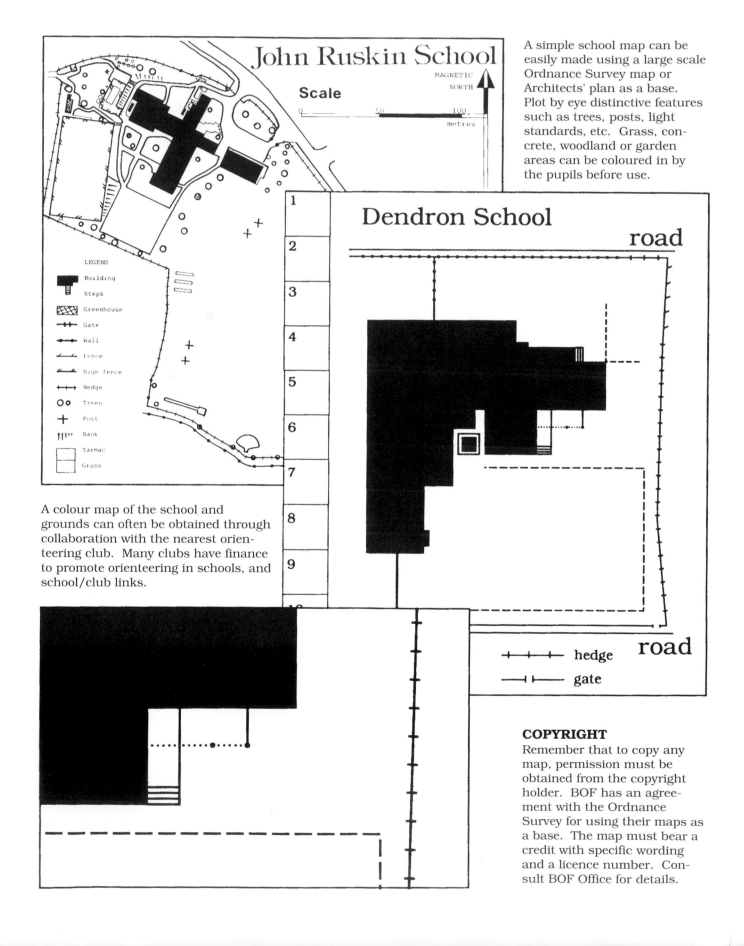

A simple school map can be easily made using a large scale Ordnance Survey map or Architects' plan as a base. Plot by eye distinctive features such as trees, posts, light standards, etc. Grass, concrete, woodland or garden areas can be coloured in by the pupils before use.

A colour map of the school and grounds can often be obtained through collaboration with the nearest orienteering club. Many clubs have finance to promote orienteering in schools, and school/club links.

John Ruskin School

Scale

MAGNETIC NORTH

0   50   100

metres

LEGEND

Building
Steps
Greenhouse
Gate
Wall
Fence
High fence
Hedge
Trees
Post
Bank
Tarmac
Grass

Dendron School

road

road

+—+—+ hedge

—I—I— gate

COPYRIGHT

Remember that to copy any map, permission must be obtained from the copyright holder. BOF has an agreement with the Ordnance Survey for using their maps as a base. The map must bear a credit with specific wording and a licence number. Consult BOF Office for details.

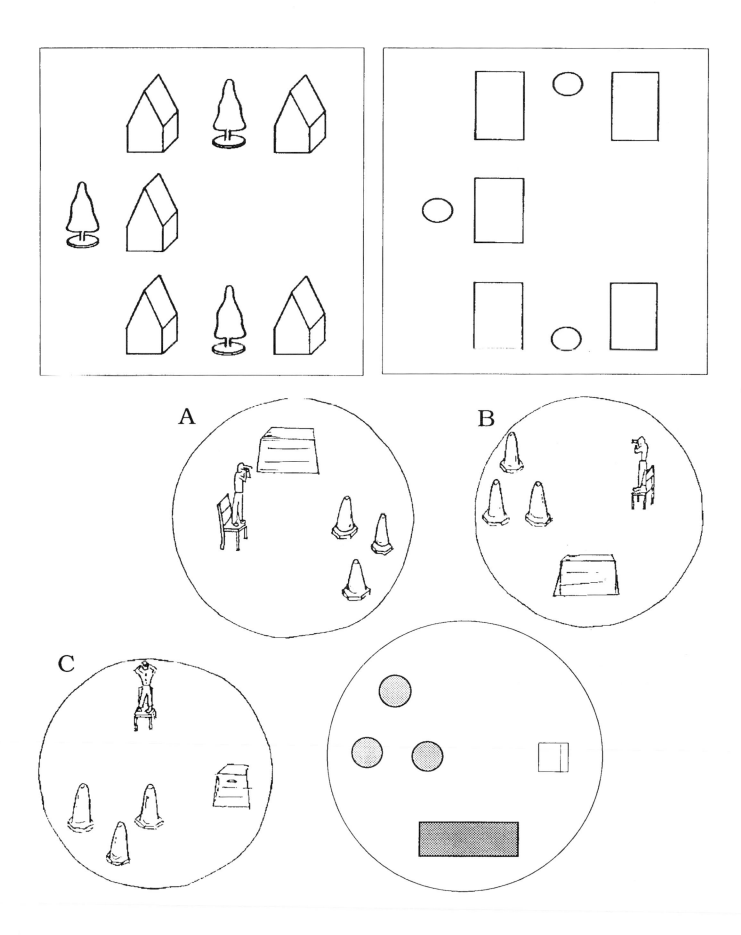

MAPS, GLOSSARY

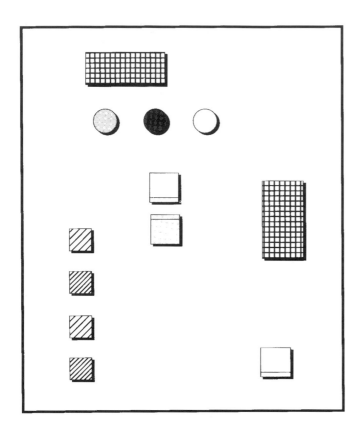

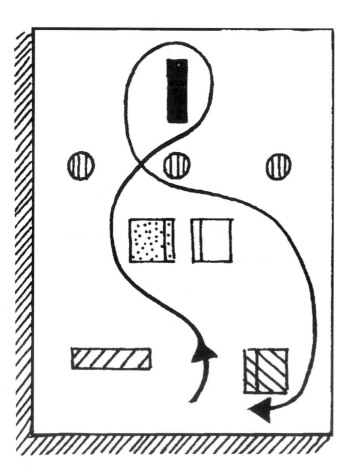

CONTROL

This is the control site, identified on the map as the centre of a circle, and on the ground by a control marker. The standard marker is three sided, orange-red and white divided diagonally, size 30 x 30cm. "Mini" (10cm square) and "micro" (4cm) markers are used for playground and indoor orienteering games.

CROSS-COUNTRY ORIENTEERING

This is the most ususal type of orienteering. The competitor must visit all the controls in a given order. Sometimes called "point to point orienteering".

MAPS AND PLANS

A map is a representation of an area, at a given scale, usually involving a degree of generalisation. There is a wide use of symbols. A symbol often takes up more space on the map than the feature would if drawn accurately to scale.

A plan is a large scale drawing. As on a map the features are shown in correct relationship but sizes and proportions are accurately scaled down.

The concepts are closely linked. A map of a play-ground may be very similar to the architect's plan.

Plans are used in most of the lessons, but are fre-quently called maps in order to make a link with maps, map reading and maps for orienteering.

ORIENTEERING

is a sport in which the competitor visits a number of points marked on the ground (controls) in the shortest possible time aided only by map and compass

SCORE ORIENTEERING

Each control is worth a number of points. The com-petition is to see how many points can be collected within a time limit by visiting as many controls as possible. The controls can be visited in any order. Exceeding the time limit attracts penalty points.

SET or ORIENTATE

To hold the map so that the features on it remain in the correct relationship to the area or landscape it represents. Setting the map is turning it the right way round so that the features in front of you on the ground are those that are in front of you on the map. When you move, in order to keep the map set, it is the body that moves.